For Mike, Katie, and Maddie, who always reach for the stars, and Rex, who's gone above and beyond. — LC

For my two little sweethearts, Tosia and Grzesui. — MN

MOON
EARTH

YOU ARE HERE

By Lisha Cauthen
Illustrator Martyna Nejman

You are here, on Earth, a just-right planet.

YOU ARE HERE
MY PLANET
EARTH
MOON

Our Earth is in just the right place in space to have liquid water and mild temperatures.

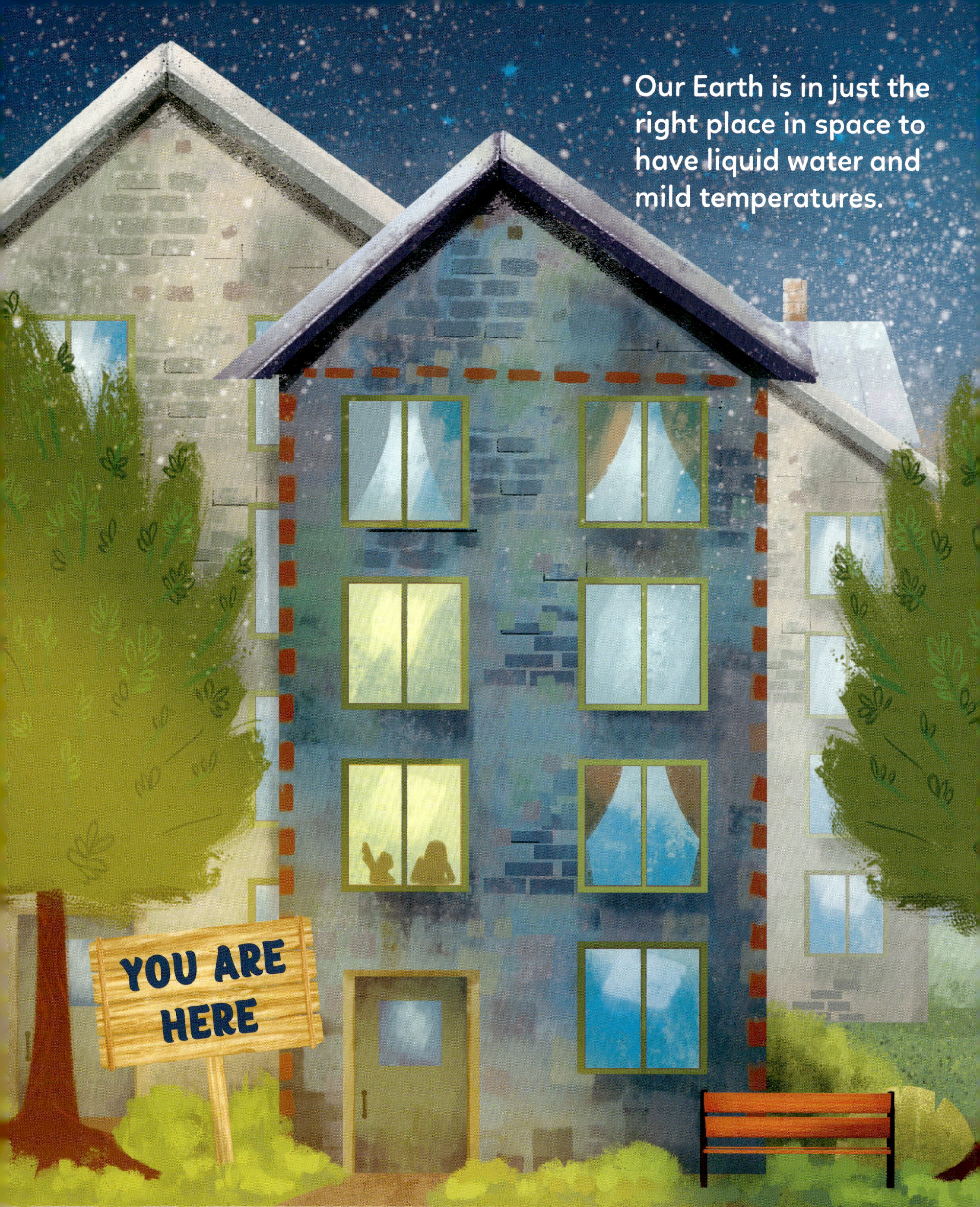

Earth's atmosphere provides oxygen for you to breathe, holds in warmth, and keeps out radiation and meteors.

Our Earth is not too far from and not too close to the sun, so it is called a Goldilocks planet. It is just right.

Our moon is a natural satellite, a rocky object that orbits a planet. Our moon doesn't have an atmosphere or liquid water. When you look at the moon, you are looking at rock that used to be part of Earth.

YOU ARE
HERE

Our sun is a yellow dwarf star, a hot ball of gas that burns in space. Stars make energy and come in different shapes, sizes, and colors.

Our Earth is much closer to our sun than any other star, but it still takes eight minutes for the sun's light to reach us.

Blue stars are the hottest stars. Red stars are the least hot. Stars can be dwarfs, giants, or supergiants.

The sun is so big, its gravity holds our whole solar system together.

Our solar system is the sun and all the planets, moons, asteroids, meteoroids, comets, gases, and space rubble that orbit or travel around the sun.

Uranus – spins on its side
7
Saturn – made of gas – can float on water
6
Jupiter – largest planet – Great Red Spot is an ancient, swirling storm
5
Neptune – farthest from the sun – the coldest planet
8

An asteroid is a large rock that orbits the sun. A meteoroid is a small rock that orbits the sun. Most asteroids and meteoroids come from the asteroid belt, which is a field of rocky debris that orbits the sun between Mars and Jupiter.

If you are the first to discover an asteroid, you can name it! Some asteroid names are Misterrogers, Muchachos, and Pinocchio.

A comet is an orbiting ice ball made of frozen gas, dust, and rock. When a comet nears the sun, it melts a little and forms two tails. One tail is made of water vapor and the other tail is made of dust.

Most comets come from the Kuiper Belt, a field of icy rock out beyond Neptune that orbits the sun. The dwarf planets Pluto and Eris are found in the Kuiper Belt.

Our galaxy is the Milky Way, which contains between 200 billion and 400 billion stars and all their planets, moons, asteroids, meteoroids, comets, gases, and space rubble.

All the stars we see in the night sky are in the Milky Way Galaxy.

Long ago, sky watchers connected the dots between stars to make imaginary pictures called constellations. These constellations have names like Ursa Major—The Great Bear, Taurus—The Bull, and Orion—The Hunter. We live in the Orion arm of the Milky Way Galaxy.

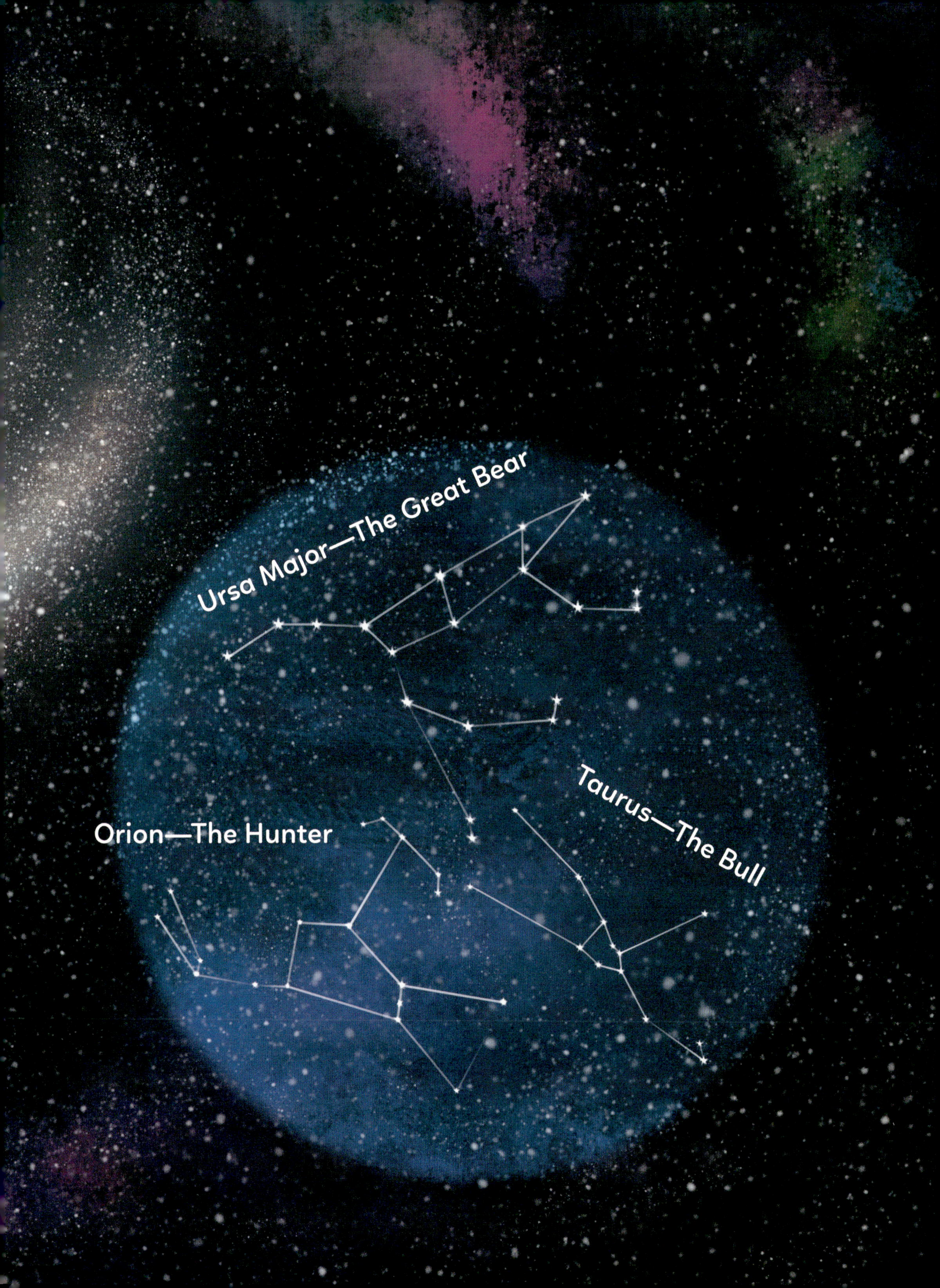
Ursa Major—The Great Bear
Orion—The Hunter
Taurus—The Bull

Our Universe is bigger than anyone knows. The longer we look, the bigger it seems. The Universe holds billions of galaxies, which contain billions and billions of stars, many with solar systems with planets, moons, asteroids, meteoroids, comets, gases, and space rubble.

Our Universe holds everything that is...

YOU ARE
HERE

and you are here.

The Universe We Cannot See

Only five percent of the universe is **bright matter**. Bright matter is all the stars, planets, moons, asteroids, meteoroids, comets, gases, and space rubble we can see. The other ninety-five percent of the universe is made up of dark energy, dark matter, and black holes.

Dark energy is the force that makes the universe expand. Scientists do not know what dark energy is, nor do they understand how it works. They know that dark energy exists because the universe we can see is expanding much faster than can be explained by gravity.

Dark matter is a physical mass that takes up space and has weight but does not give off light. Scientists do not know what dark matter is, but they know it exists because galaxies behave as if they contain more matter than we can see.

A black hole is an enormous amount of matter crammed into a small area. Because a black hole is so dense, its gravitational pull is extremely strong. This strong gravitational pull does not allow anything to escape the black hole, including light. We know that black holes exist because we can see how their presence changes the space that surrounds them. Black holes pull in matter such as gas, dust, stars, and other black holes. Most galaxies have black holes at their center, which were formed at the same time as the galaxy. Some black holes are collapsed stars. Some black holes can be the size of a solar system. Other black holes are the size of one atom.

Astronomers are scientists who constantly search space and perform experiments to understand how our universe works. New discoveries happen every day!

Bibliography

Anderson, Amy, and Brian Anderson Ph.D. **Space Dictionary For Kids: The Everything Guide For Kids Who Love Space.** Prufrock Press Inc., 2016.

Bingham, Caroline. **First Space Encyclopedia.** DK Publishing Inc., 2008.

Buckley, James Jr. **Stars and Galaxies.** DK Publishing, 2017.

Crane, Cody. **The Stars.** Children's Press, Imprint of Scholastic, 2018.

Goldsmith, Dr. Mike, and Jacqueline Mitton. **Amazing Space Q&A.** DK Publishing, 2011.

Lippincott, Kristen. **Eyewitness Astronomy.** DK Publishing, 2013.

NASA Science. https://science.nasa.gov/. Accessed 2019.

NASA Space Place. https://spaceplace.nasa.gov/. Accessed 2019.

Stars—Birth and Death, World Book Inc., 2017.

Library of Congress Cataloging-in-Publication Data available

ISBN 978-1-63333-058-0

Published by

the little fig®

www.thelittlefig.com